Thunderstorm of Emotions

Danielle Jassie

BookLeaf Publishing

Presentation by *BookLeaf Publishing*

Web: www.bookleafpub.com

E-mail: info@bookleafpub.com

ISBN: 978-93-5744-342-5

First edition 2022

DEDICATION

I dedicate this book to my mum,

Sarah Chafer.

1969-2014

Alone

They all stare as you walk by,
They wonder and want to learn,
Do you want to help the world bloom
Or will you stand and watch it burn?

Am I with them or with you?
I try keep my mind open,
But they all talk so loud
And I can't help being roped in.

I don't want to be alone,
But I don't know who to trust.
How do I continue
Without going bust?

I'll find my way forward
And listen to my heart,
I'll block out the chatter
And make a fresh start.

Struggling

It’s getting harder every day
To be restless in my bed,
And make the choice to stay,
With my head filled with dread.

There’s been way too much abuse,
That’s why I’m holding on to you.
You need to keep me safe,
Be the home I always knew.

But now it’s starting to come back,
And it seems you're starting to lack
Your care and love to me.
It’s making my heart crack.

Women's pain

From a teenage girl
They always say
‘Most woman feel pain,
That’s just it’s way’

So you try to listen
But your doubt is sure,
‘Its too much pain
For me to endure’.

You try to pretend
You try to be fine,
You don’t want to fuss,
Or grumble or whine.

But you need to be clear,
'Cause it can’t be routine,
For every woman to sting
'Til aged from their teens.

Hurry to the doctor,
And voice your pain loud,
'Cause they don’t always catch it
The first time around.

Don’t stay in agony,
No matter what they claim,
It’s just not normal
To be in so much pain.

Quiet

Rarely alone,
But never heard.
They never hear
A single word

I try be loud,
Don't think I'm quiet,
But I'm surrounded
By a riot.

I fade away
Into the crowd,
No matter if
I think I'm loud.

Would anyone notice
If I wasn't here?
Don't think they would,
That's what I fear.

The fire inside

I’ve endured so much hardship
In just a few years
And it started a storm
From all of my fears

To the world and all of life
My anger does burn
For those that they’ve taken
My heart does yearn

I don’t mean to hurt others
I try control the flames
But the fight tires me
And I'm forced to play its games.

Gone, but not lost

Life is short
That's what you taught
When you faded too soon
And I try
Not to cry
When I see you in the moon

I see you there
In the glare
Of every ray of sunlight
You watch us go
Through high and low
And push on with all our might

Our family's broken
'Cause you were our token
That kept us all together
But we try to carry on
Through every dusk and dawn
As you guide through stormy weather.

You were always there
To help us bear
Any trouble that we found.
And now from above
We still feel your love
As we trudge upon the ground.

No win, all lose

You throw a tantrum
And think you win.
You think me dumb
And this is fin.

You cannot break me,
I will not yield.
Just wait and see
Once my wounds have healed.

I'll be up once again
And I will defy.
No matter the strain
I'll always try.

For now, you prevail,
But soon you'll realise,
You ultimately fail
From all those white lies.

Constant War

Are my efforts for nil?
I won't know until,
We have victory or defeat.

But why should I
Continue to fight
When my comrade will not battle?

An army of one
Is as good as done,
As the brawl will surely vanquish.

I'll continue the scrimmage,
And keep up our image,
And hope it'll be enough.

Comfort Zone

You run and hide from the world,
But where in the world can you hide?
You cower away from the dark,
So no one sees when you've cried.

Things may seem bleak now,
But nevertheless
There will always be a haven
You can access.

But You can't stay forever
In your comfort zone.
You may be safe,
But you'll end up alone.

There will come a time
To face the sorrow.
You must trust you are enough
And will be smiling tomorrow.

Endless Anguish

Your mind's a muddle,
Thoughts are in disarray,
You try to organise
But they keep going stray.

You're terrified and unsure.
You cower, try to hide.
It can be frightening
Not knowing your own mind.

One misguided word
Can send you back in time,
To a scene you mustn't relive,
But it still echoes and chimes.

Despite your efforts,
It just won't stop.
Keeps haunting you
Until the tears drop.

You're not alone
In being troubled by the past.
You can get through it,
And be free at last.

Temptations

Torn two ways,
Commit sin, or be saint.
Living two lives,
One being just a feint.

Fail to ignore
The whispers from my Id,
But I'm allured
And down the slope, I slid.

Filled with guilt,
But also wicked thrill,
That I'll soon regret,
I just know I will.

The buzz is gone.
Back to reality.
I'll be tempted once more,
When I need to feel free.

Separated

They run and laugh
And play their games,
But you miss it all,
And get all the blame.

You work hard to see
Each smile on their face,
As you peer at each photo,
Which holds your empty space.

You say it'll get better,
And someday soon,
You'll be there with them,
Through September from June.

Keep hoping it will
And work towards that goal,
Until you can hold them in your arms,
And once again feel whole.

Comfort Pet

At the end of a dreary day,
When I'm weary with lots to say,
I go to my room where you wait,
And look into your furry face.

A comfort pet when I'm in need,
When we met you planted a seed,
Deep in my heart and, I hope, in yours,
Lie with me and keep each other warm.

In the morning after an endless night,
I feel you close and hold you tight.
I dry my tears and prepare myself,
'Cause you need me to stay in good health.

A comfort pet for when I'm in need,
But there's more than that that others see,
Because you care for me while I care for you,
You're not just a pet but a best friend, it's true.

Breaking Point

Don't be ashamed
To give yourself a break,
Because life has given
More than you can take.

You may be tired,
Over-stressed and drained.
Let yourself rest
To become unchained.

For any single person,
There's nothing that you owe.
Just care for yourself,
So that you may glow.

Conform

When life is dull and grey,
And they all keep to the routine,
Of sleep, eat, work, repeat,
Just escape and create your own scene.

Add bubbles to the thunder,
And flavour to the bland.
Keep colour in your corner,
And don’t get buried in the sand.

Be the sparkle in the night,
And the dancer in the rain,
When the world pushes down
And just tries to cause you pain.

Don't let them tie you down
And follow with the horde.
Let yourself be free
To jump and dance and soar.

Royalty

Wipe away the tears,
And hold your head up high.
Collect the broken pieces,
And throw them to the sky.

You can be royalty.
Just keep your self-esteem
On the highest podium,
And just watch it as it gleams.

Hope

Feeling empty and so numb
Craving the touch of anyone
But even while filled with fright
I'll keep looking for the light.

I know it's there, just needs a spark
Something deep, close to my heart
I might be wrong, but I've had a clue,
But what kept me going was always you.

Keep going

Each and every one of us
Can often feel life's bane.
Most of us keep on trying
And try ignore the pain.

Not all will feel as strong
And tiptoe to the brink,
But we all will have a reason
To step away and think,

Even if not now,
It will be worth the while
To keep on going another day
And soon again, I'll smile.'

Each day that you face
When you think you can't persist,
Will always be a victory,
And one that shan't be missed.

www.ingramcontent.com/pod-product-compliance
Lightning Source LLC
Chambersburg PA
CBHW051720130826
49812CB00034B/1275
9789357443425